# Black Lives Matter!

## AN EMERGENCY RESPONSE TO CRISIS

### JAMES P. QUINCY, III

*Waterfall Publishing*
*Cleveland, Ohio*

Black Lives Matter
An Emergency Response to Crisis
Copyright © 2015 by James P. Quincy, III

cover art by Neomedia Group, Atlanta, GA

Printed in the United States of America

All Rights Reserved
No part of this publication may be reproduced, stored in a retrieval system, or transmitted, in any form or by any means—electronic, mechanical, photocopying, recording or otherwise—without prior written permission.

ISBN: 978-0-9729576-3-2

For information:

Waterfall Publishing
Cleveland, Ohio 44128

# Contents

| | |
|---|---|
| Dedication | 5 |
| Acknowledgement | 7 |
| Introduction | 9 |
| The Crisis of Valuation | 13 |
| Inspire Black Lives | 21 |
| Respect Black Lives | 27 |
| Love Black Lives | 33 |
| Educate Black Lives | 39 |
| Engage Black Lives | 45 |
| Protect Black Lives – Election Day | 55 |
| Protect Black Lives – Judgment Day | 63 |
| Lives Matter | 69 |
| Black Men Respond | 73 |
| Epilogue | 85 |

# Dedication

*Dedicated to those who have defeated odds to overcome challenges, statistics and stereotypes; and to mothers and fathers who have mourned their young much too soon.*

6

# Acknowledgement

This book was difficult to write because the wounds are so fresh and common. It was necessary to approach this topic for the very same reasons. There is so much pain left by the common occurrences of tragic violence in the urban community. It is essential that we respond to the low-level value placed on the lives of too many American children. This was difficult because it is a direct response to a number of months of active protests to grand jury actions around cases of alleged misconduct by police officers in Ferguson, Missouri and New York City.

During the same period, a twelve year old was shot and killed by a police officer in Cleveland. My attempt to respond to this "crisis" in our nation became further convoluted when two New York City police officers were gunned down sitting in their patrol car in broad daylight on a Brooklyn street in New York City. To say that "lives matter" and not to acknowledge the pain and suffering of these families would be a stoic contradiction.

I firmly believe that all lives matter and have deep value, especially those that find themselves in the middle of our national conversations and divisions over race, power and privilege. I am extremely perplexed by the unwarranted killing of unarmed individuals within our communities. Yet, I am equally disturbed by execution-style murders of police officers, prosecutors, and other public servants, who during the course of their service to humanity lose their lives. We must work to achieve a society where people are treated with respect and the dissemination of force is both warranted and just.

James Quincy
January, 2015

# *Introduction*

When I received the call that two New York City police officers had been gunned down in their patrol car on the Saturday before Christmas it gripped me deeply. This transpired right in the middle of protests occurring nationally to highlight the killing of black males by police. It did not provide comfort or appeasement to the protesters or their causes. It was further proof that our system of values is broken. Killing is not only contrary to Biblical principles, but it devastates families and communities. All life is essentially worth living and all life matters. It is our collective responsibility to make this point as clearly as possible. It is also our collective responsibility to live in such a way that we feel the importance of all human life and are willing to protect it at all costs. We are too quick to turn our backs, our hands, and our resources away from the casual reality that life does not matter—all life matters. It must be stated that this is not a given.

The recent militarization of our nation's police forces has only heightened the abuse of power and implementation of "police states" in major cities. The deaths of men and women at the hands of the public servants who are sworn to protect them strikes a particular irony. The repeated press conferences, grand jury events and civil disobedience that follow have left a bitter taste in the mouth of Lady Justice. They have left mothers and communities crying out for answers in the midst of their mourning and pain. The answers come too few and too far in between. The result is that in city after city communities are ripped apart trying to sort through the untimely grief that exposes the inequalities in our system of justice.

The primary objective of this book is to present a response to the "crisis" of unequal justice in our policing practices in the United Sates. This response intends to provide some principles for improving the valuation of black lives in America. It is abundantly clear that this "crisis" is not limited to black lives or that only those lives taken by police matter. People of color across the board are disproportionately impacted by police militarization and misconduct, however, I have purposely used black lives for this discussion with no attempt to limit or minimalize the broader impact.

Crime is an awful reality around the world. From white collar corruption to street-level corruption, crime devastates communities and lives. The need for policing agencies remains very high and the men and women who serve are very courageous. They too require appropriate protection because all lives matter. As a basic premise, it is important to stress that police are not the enemies. The enemy is injustice, inequality and disproportionate use of force. Our response must be a response that addresses the individual and collect understanding that young black lives matter. In fact, to make it clear – all lives matter.

# The Crisis of Valuation

## Chapter One

The United States of America is possibly the greatest experiment in nation development that the world has ever seen.  This is not to say that our nation is the greatest nation that has ever existed.  It is to say that the foundational principles and construction of this nation are incredible even in light of all its problems since the arrival of the first men from England.  This development has always been an experiment with challenges, atrocities, heroism and inequality.  I guess that this is what makes this experiment so intriguing.  It is intriguing because our stated goals are freedom and equality and yet with the very first settlers came inequality and injustice.  But, we still love this country, because foundationally we believe in the equality of all—not seen, not felt, and perhaps never to be.

As I write this I do so primarily from an urban African American perspective. As much as I approach this conversation from that perspective, I am fully aware of the fact that people of color across this nation are often impacted similarly. To the extent that we can raise the conscious level, I hope that we can feel the lifting of unnecessary oppression, injustice and burden of race from all Americans. I pray that we can truly live out the creed of our nation, notwithstanding its past transgressions. If we can repair the breach and commence living the "Golden Rule" as articulated in the Gospel of Matthew, we may achieve the foundational goals of our democracy and the founders who meant well and believed in its future.

For over twenty years I have been responding to the crisis of Ferguson and working to protect the lives of young black and brown men and women. The concept of "black lives matter" has been a staple in my work and development over the past three decades. It started when I was a freshman in high school and I ran for class president. It was an election that I lost. I lost that election because I was considered to be too square and even a teacher's pet. The problem with that thinking—then and now—is that it keeps our young black men from achieving and excelling. I responded as any fourteen-year-old would, I toned down my enthusiasm for academic success and raised my social profile. As a result, I was elected president the next year and succeeded in student politics in high school, college and graduate school. Now, thanks to my mother, I didn't fully abandon my academic pursuits and went to some of the top colleges in America. My point is that my fight for black youth and black life started right there at Inkster High School.

The crisis affecting African American males in this country is not a new concept. We can go back and review the number of historical areas where African American males have been sacrificed at the hands of a nation that really ought to be truly grateful to the black male. From the impact of the black male on the development of the American economy during the slavocracy to the night shift at almost any major retailer for minimum wage in 2015, the development of the American economy owes a debt of gratitude to the black male. If I spent enough time, I could make that point through a review of the civil war, the civil rights movement, the Vietnam War, and multiple wars in the Middle East. Yet, consistently, this part of our population has been ostracized, criticized, demonized and systematically eliminated.

My point in this writing is not to suggest or diminish in any way the contributions made by so many other components in the American experience, but I am making the point that we undervalue the lives of black males and have done so for centuries. So, our response to the devaluation of black males must be consistent, calculated and coordinated. Over the past few weeks, months and years I've watched the reaction to the untimely, unwarranted and unnecessary deaths of black men. From massive protests a few years ago in the death of Trayvon Martin, Jordan Davis, and the "Jena Six" to Michael Brown, Tamir Rice, and Eric Garner in 2014. Our responses are too often short lived and our responsibility between crises dwindles and fades away. Now, I'm not advocating for a continuous onslaught of massive protests across the country, I'm really advocating for action. Following are six points that I believe can aid a systematic and calculated attempt to strengthen black males and inspire them to seek and achieve the greatness that was planted in them by their creator.

    The time has come for someone to offer some concrete suggestions that will do more than raise consciousness. We need some real-time, real-life practices that everyone can implement to make a difference before more lives are lost.  Simply instructing our children on proper conduct when approached by law-enforcement is not enough.  Our need is to loudly proclaim that all life matters.  This message is not only a message for law enforcement, but for offenders, criminals and young people themselves.  If our young people are not taught that their lives are of value and that other lives matter as well this cycle is bound to repeat itself.  If that occurs we must prepare to witness the escalation of unwarranted, untimely, and unnecessary losses.

    We could wax philosophically, spiritually, or politically about this issue for hours, we can debate its merits and causes and we could spend days placing and assessing blame of party, race, or history.  The reality is that the concept of creating a culture where black lives matter is impossible within a culture that devalues lives in general.  We must effectively, consistently and concretely address the issues and concerns that are foundational in the valuation of lives, in general and young black male lives in particular. This starts with a paradigm shift in our minds that flows through our spiritual and mental faculties, which results in a change in behavior.

I am suggesting a shift from being simply reactionary to raising our degrees of prevention. I purposely meander through my journey as a young black man through the journeys of others and the work that we have done throughout the United States to help young people raise their view of self and the value that they place on their lives and the lives of others. I share six specific points to ensure that black lives matter. These points are inspiration, education, love, respect, participation, and protection.

# Inspire Black Lives

## Chapter Two

In 1993, I was invited to join the staff at Calvary Baptist Church in Jamaica, New York by the Rev. Victor T. Hall, Sr. This was a time when rap music had accelerated its influence and the hip hop generation was finding their footing. Our task then was to work to address the valuation of the black male. To be clear, it was not defined as such back then, yet in retrospect that is exactly what we were called to do and exactly what we did. We engaged hundreds of black males and challenged them to consider their lives in a very different way. Through a number of activities, engagements, and challenges, we took young males who were considered destined for death and jail and provided them with the inspiration, desire and tools to be great. To say they responded would be an understatement. Today, many of those boys are now men with positive lives and promising futures.

We invested in a number of activities to inspire young people to become great. We invested in academics, recreation, and personal responsibility among other attributes. In one example, twelve young black adolescent males were challenged to provide leadership for their peers. They were challenged to study God's word on a level that would rival a first year seminary student. They were challenged in their academics as we required weekly progress reports from their schools. They were challenged to consider the impact, consequences and circumstances of what we called "too early sexual activity." In responding to the challenge they and others provided leadership for their local church, their community and ultimately throughout New York State. Today, they continue to lead in ministry, industry and community service.

Another example was the formulation of a church basketball league, which brought fourteen new churches together with thirteen existing basketball teams. The result was that hundreds of young black and Hispanic boys and girls were provided with a positive platform to enhance their social, physical and spiritual development. The impact was phenomenal. At least one of these students, Royal Ivey, spent a decade in the National Basketball Association. Today, others are fathers, ministers, police officers, and a myriad of other positive accomplishments.

Inspiration is a very important step in the process of optimizing the valuation of black lives. Yes, black lives matter and inspiration is a great way to perpetuate that reality. I am convinced that inspiration is one of the major concepts absent in young black males and the result is a devaluation of self. This devaluation of self is actually far more damaging than many external factors that threaten black males. Inspiration is a powerful concept that is so infrequently instilled. I believe that one of the reasons so many African Americans succeeded prior to and during the civil rights era is that they were constantly inspired to succeed. They were taught the high importance of education, the value of hard work and the importance of never giving up. The extent to which we continue this tradition of inspiring the next generation is a good measuring stick for the trajectory of life. The ability to place significant value on life—your life—increases the odds that you will protect that life. The value of a watch is likely to determine the level of care taken in protecting it from loss or damage.

Inspiration is one of my six themes which can be done on a daily and consistent basis. Individually, we can work to inspire the next generation regularly. Everyone can be told what they can't do; it is rare that young people are challenged with what they can do. In other words, a caring loving adult can often see the potential that the young person cannot see within himself. Too often, we skip this opportunity because of fear of retribution or rejection. I can tell you that students still respond to motivation, stimulation and encouragement. Students are still willing to increase their self-estimate or personal valuation. The reality is that the media, society, and even family has a tendency to reemphasize the lower valuation of black lives and many black males simply do not believe that their lives matter and frankly neither do we. Inspire greatness.

# Respect Black Lives

## Chapter Three

In 2001, I was invited to join the staff at First Baptist Institutional Church in Detroit under the leadership of Rev. Howard B.M. Fauntroy, Jr. What an amazing time this was during the advent of social media and students becoming more Internet savvy. Yet, during that period Detroit's literacy rate was deplorable and the digital divide was in full swing. Our goal was to embrace a neighborhood full of children. We opened our doors and our hearts to that community and found an overwhelming response. During my five years there hundreds of students visited the church, played basketball, studied the Bible, engaged in homework, met the mayor's staff, and were loved. These students didn't move into the neighborhood—they lived there. But, the love of a cup of hot chocolate in the winter or a cold Gatorade during the summer changed their relationship to the body and ultimately gave them a new self-image and personal valuation.

We developed a computer center in the church to attack illiteracy and the digital divide simultaneously. Each student was required to create an email address, which was major at this point in time. They were provided access to the center on a daily basis to do homework, surf the web and to develop reading, writing and comprehension skills. Our team volunteered their time and expertise to develop and train these young minds.

Another example was the work of tilling soil and planting the produce in our garden, which interestingly enough, forced us to relocate the basketball rim. The garden was an excellent opportunity to deepen the concept of respect for self, nature and God. The students learned to plant, nurture and ultimately harvested some fresh produce. Among the vast array of educational, social and spiritual programs was the S.T.O.R.E. Adopted from Calvary Baptist Church, the Student Team On

Reinvestment Economics developed an in-house shop for students to get snacks rather than going to the corner store. The profit from the sale of products was reinvested into the youth program for the students.

Our team sincerely loved these students and reached out to them. They were exposed to places they had only heard others talk about. Visits to New York, Washington, D.C. and South Africa exposed them to greater possibilities and realities for their lives. It was just that simple, but not simply that. The students were treated with a tremendous amount of love both at home and when they traveled. They received encouraging words, material gifts and an abundance of encouragement, discipline and exposure. If black lives matter, then we ought to love them completely and unconditionally. We can't only love them when they are no longer alive; we have to honor them while they are still around. We must love them when they don't feel as if they can be loved and we must love the seemingly unlovable. Teenagers can be hard to love sometimes, but that's exactly when they need to be loved. Our love for them must be constant and visible when they can see it and feel it. After they have been eulogized and laid to rest is too late. Hold up a picture of a black life that is still alive from time to time. Let's make some facial placards of some young people in our neighborhoods, schools and congregations while they are still alive and can see and feel the love and be inspired by it.

One student came in with a level of curiosity about his younger twin brothers' involvement at the church. As we began to talk he boldly proclaimed that he was a Muslim. I said "really, what branch of Islam?" He was obviously not expecting that response, but I was determined to respect his position in life. After additional conversation he left, unconverted. But, the love, inspiration and respect that were shared with him on that day led him back. Each time he came, he learned more. Ultimately, he converted, joined and later became youth president. If black lives matter—they must be respected. If we work to respect young black men, we potentially gain their ear and ultimately their hearts. Let's face it—we live in a society that rarely demonstrates respect for any black man—not to mention an eighteen year old black life. This would be the perfect place to launch into a discussion of the treatment of President Barack Obama, but I will let that stand. We increase the valuation of black lives when we let black children know that they are respected and loved. I've been taught and have taught that "respect begets respect," that is respect for others produces respect for you. We want young people to respect us—let us make a conscious effort to respect black lives daily as we honor the value of life.

# Love Black Lives

## Chapter Four

In 2007, I travelled to South Africa to serve as the acting pastor for the Tabernacle Church of God in Christ in Ivory Park outside of Johannesburg. I was invited by Pastors Vincent and Sharon Mathews. My responsibility was to maintain the ministries, preach, teach and provide pastoral care during the period of the pastors' absence in the United States. This experience was truly a labor of love and I received so much love in return. My goal was to bring Christmas to the children of the church during my month-long stay. As one of America's premiere youth pastors, I was challenged to make an impact on these young people in a short amount of time.

We went straight to work, training youth workers using my own book *May I Help You* and Doug Field's book *Purpose Driven Youth Ministry*. We also kicked off several programs for youth and children that were rooted in love. That is we spent time with them, shared snacks with them and literally rolled through yard with them. I found myself on any given day surrounded by little children, who did not have shoes on their feet, but they felt our love. We did what the Bible taught; fed the hungry, clothed the naked, and loved the children—unconditionally. They had nothing to give or to offer and could have easily been ignored. Thanks to the generosity of many from the United States, we were able to purchase "black" dolls for the girls; marbles, soccer balls and cars for the boys; and books for everyone. It was great to see the young people celebrating Christmas and being encouraged by the love of strangers thousands of miles away.

In addition to the training and the activities, we turned an unused wing into a vibrant youth center with bright colors and synthetic flowers. There were a few young adults who cared enough to remove the old debris and with great sweat equity removed years of soil. Ultimately, they found a way to make the concrete shine as if immaculately and professionally waxed.

It was not a grand investment of state funds or some grant that paid for service and construction. It was men and women who cared enough to use what they had to show their unconditional love for the children of that community. Soon after the work was completed, hundreds of children, youth and young adults found refuge, fellowship and encouragement during those hot summer days. It was a great experience of love and commitment.

It is important to make sure that children of color are given suitable and bountiful quantities of love. Society today has constantly taught our children that they are unlovable and devoid of the concepts of love. The images and stereotypes that are often conveyed and engrained in young minds begin to shape their lives from a very young age. Our job is to work to demonstrate and practice a deep level of love and affection in an effort to reverse the emotional impact that these images have on our children. That love includes both spoken and felt love. Working to intentionally teach the love of God and express that love in appropriate ways is an essential component to helping to ensure that black lives matter.

The unconditional love of Jesus allows us to love ourselves through an understanding of our value on a cosmic level. The truth that God, through Jesus, has instilled love within each individual will work to automatically increase one's value of self. I am convinced that we are challenged to appropriately value others when we fail to value ourselves. Black lives matter when they feel and express love. Not just a sensual exhibition of love, but the true unconditional love that comes from a deeper understanding and relationship with God.

Teachers must love their students enough to provide premium education, even in substandard conditions. This is how a "separate but equal" educational system in the United States could produce so many men and women of color who valued and fought for educational freedoms in this nation. Preachers must love enough to minister to the needs of people, by serving communities from a foundational position of spiritual responsibility and not simply out of popularity and one's willingness to make sacrifices. When I consider the sacrifice of Jesus between two thieves on a cross in the desert Middle East and how maintaining an unpopular and unpleasant position was what He came to do, I am reminded that I can never out give Jesus. The good thing is that we are not called to give more—but to give what we can—love.

For example, as we meet the direct needs of children we demonstrate love. But, our love must not be limited to material support. It is the time we spend, the ears we lend and the comfort of our presence that implants their emotions with love. To convince this generation that their lives matter will take an all-out commitment of unconditional love that encompasses more than material gifts. Our commitments of time and encouragement will go so much farther than our material investments. Appropriate unconditional love from black men, in particular, investing time and energy in the lives of young people, will demonstrate that their lives matter.

# Educate Black Lives

## Chapter Five

In 2013, I was called to serve as Pastor of Lee Road Baptist Church in Cleveland. Our congregation is relatively diverse, yet the largest demographic in our church is retired educators. This is a tremendous benefit because they understand the value of educating the next generation. Education is one of the most essential tools in increasing self-esteem and personal valuation. It is because black lives matter that we are challenged to educate them and inspire them. Black lives matter because they are lives, but with education they are given a greater chance to navigate and manage those lives. It is clear that so much of our lives are given to economic factors and a great deal of what drives personal economy, especially for African Americans, is education. Our students require educational opportunities that will provide them with the pride and dignity that allows them to walk with their heads up and not down. We must reject the "anti-education" rhetoric with which we develop young black boys. This is not a concept that begins with students in the schools or outside the homes. Unfortunately, it is clearly a concept that is fostered in our community. Young black males need adults who regularly and consistently promote positive educational advancement for boys and girls.

We decided, with the guidance of Youth Advocate, Gail Reese, to adopt John F. Kennedy High School. The school is phasing out the traditional education model and implementing a more advanced integrated program. Our members support athletic events, monitor lunch hours, and support the overall direction of the staff. We pray for the school and encourage individual students. It is a promising way to promote education by meeting students where they are—in their schools. We also invest in students through scholarships to incoming and returning students. As well, when they come home for college break, we bring the high school and college students together to discuss their experiences and expectations. We also bring in professionals to share their experiences with our students.

Involvement in the educational development of students is an essential part of my six point plan. I'm talking about far more than making students go to school and checking homework, though those things are important tasks. We must also encourage and expect excellence while enhancing the potential for excellence. We must spend some time in a school each semester to encourage and develop education in young people. There are so many options. You can go into a school and read to students, monitor lunch, speak at career days and college fairs, or perhaps donate books, uniforms, supplies or instruments. There are a number of ways to get involved. Perhaps you can volunteer in tutoring or homework help at your church. For years, I went into the public schools in Boston, Cambridge, Detroit, New York and Inkster, Michigan to engage students in civic responsibility. The schools were welcoming and the students were excited to learn about ways to better their own communities.

Every moment spent reversing the age-old theme that education is for someone else is priceless in the current era. The widespread anti-education, pro-street urban mentality that has reduced the value of young black lives has to be adjusted to make room for life. That is to say, that young people, who have been systematically stereotyped, categorized and devalued must be retrained, reshaped and taught that their lives matter. It is only when they realize that their lives matter that they will work harder to protect them. A dramatic shift in the hypothesis of life and living is needed to convey the very strong message that black lives matter.

44

# Engage Black Lives

## Chapter Six

# "To Protect and To Serve"

**LAPD Online:**

*In February 1955, the Los Angeles Police Department through the pages of the internally produced BEAT magazine, conducted a contest stated that: "The motto should be one that in a few words would express some or all the ideals to which the Los Angeles police service is dedicated. It is possible that the winning motto might someday be adopted as the official motto of the Department. The winning entry was the motto, "To Protect and to Serve" submitted by Officer Joseph S. Dorobek. "To Protect and to Serve" became the official motto of the Police Academy, and it was kept constantly before the officers in training as the aim and purpose of their profession. With the passing of time, the motto received wider exposure and acceptance throughout the department. On November 4, 1963, the Los Angeles City Council passed the necessary ordinance and the credo has now been placed alongside the City Seal on the Department's patrol cars.*

(http://www.lapdonline.org/history_of_the_lapd/content_basic_view/1128)

The commander of the 113th Precinct in Queens was an extremely progressive champion of community policing. He would gather members of the community in meetings and conversations, he attended various community events, he sent text messages when there was a particularly brutal crime committed, a particular alert needed to be raised or the department was preparing for a crackdown of sorts. His operational behavior engaged a community at a time when there was a huge disparity in the ethnic make-up of the precinct and the community.

The officers in the 113th Precinct were over ninety percent Caucasian and the neighborhood was over ninety percent people of color. Yet, the 113th was located just minutes away from the Belt Parkway, which took you quickly to the comforts of suburban Long Island living. The result was if you were interested in a precinct close to home, 113th was one of the closest. It was not known as one of the safest, but it was very close to Long Island.

On the occasions that I was given the opportunity to address the roll call of officers at the precinct. It was always a sea of unfamiliar faces looking forward to the end of their shift and getting home to their wives and children. My goal in addressing roll call was to put a face on the humanity of the young black lives that were about to stand in between these officers and their evening drives to Long Island. What I understood was that any impact I had in those few minutes would be minimal but could very well help to rouse caution in the minds of those officers as they engaged the arrogance of youth in the teens they would patrol. I often wondered how much different the conversation would be if those faces were black and brown.

There is a tremendous need for police officers in our society today. Admittedly, if there was an overwhelming appreciation for the value of life, we would possibly live without police. This is far from our reality and because these brave men and women put their lives on the line every day, we can generally live our lives with relative ease. The fact is that our relationship is greatly impacted by the disproportionate racial configuration of the police force and the urban communities, which desperately require them.

In a recent conversation with a veteran New York City police officer, who is African American, the dilemma was starkly clear. The quandary is being African American and understanding the distress of discrimination and oppression, while simultaneously being an officer and understanding the challenges and dangers of the job. Remarkably he loves his job and his community. He stated: "It's just like being a Christian and being saved, no one will understand you—the only job is to do what's right. You do your job out of love, commitment and obedience. It is a thankless job—that I found easy to do because I'm a Christian."

As I spoke with him and listened to him share his burden, I reflected on how unfair it is. It is absolutely unfair that there are so few black men among the ranks of police departments all across this nation. It makes their job tougher and lonely and often overly painful. I believe that so many of the police involved shootings that leave young black men wounded or dead are the result of personality conflicts and mistrust from one person to another. It really is and isn't about race. That is to say that few people would actually say that I want to kill someone of a different race, persuasion or color, simply because they are. But, many times it is the perspective from which we see "the other" that we make judgments about what we feel about that person and the proper way to respond to what we feel and what we see. As he references a recent event where he goes to pick up a child from school and upon presenting his identification—a police identification--a woman grabs her son and says, "Please, don't kill my baby." Upon inquiry she responds, "because, you all kill black men." It is not true that all police officers are killers that target black men. It is true that this distrust exists and that there is a divide that makes one suspicious of the other.

It is imperative that we develop deliberate, focused and coordinated programs to increase the number of black and brown males and females in our nation's police departments. I am convinced that an increase in black officers will bring more sensitivity to departments, impact those currently serving and force departments to evaluate their practices and procedures. Again, if the individuals who police communities exhibit a level of like-mindedness it can be that perspectives can change and long held positions about various pockets of the population can be muted and replaced with mutual understanding and respect. Mutual respect can make a critical difference when faced with critical decisions at a moment's notice.

Although this generation is far more diverse and integrated than before, the perspective and views of young people do not reflect the perspectives and views of their parents. In fact their closeness can be one of the major challenges that families face. That's why encouraging young people to consider careers in law enforcement is more important than ever. The ability to get like-minded men and women in uniform has the potential not only to decrease the ethnic disparity, but to shift the perspective by which police view the community they serve. To serve and to protect a community is about more than the weapons that are issued to ensure order, but it is about the minds that are necessary to guarantee justice. Our system of policing must shift to one that produces an organic compulsion for love of the police and their policing practices. One could imagine that the Los Angeles policeman who submitted his entry sixty years ago intended for his department to be loved and appreciated. Good policing is done when the officers are absolutely convinced that on the most difficult of days—all lives matter!

54

Protect Black Lives

Election Day

Chapter Seven

A paradigm shift in our communities can shake up our society and demonstrate that black lives matter. Voting is such a critical component of demonstrating that all lives matter. There are basically two ways to speak in American society today. One is with your money and the other is with your vote. When we fail to vote, we are silenced and silencing ourselves. In a most recent national election less than forty percent of the American people participated in the process. That means that local leaders were determined and chosen by a very small number of votes. We say "our votes don't matter," but they matter less when we do not use them. How is it possible for a community to be seventy-five percent black and have little or no black elected officials? That can only happen when the majority of voters do not participate in the process. We can't scream our way to getting others to change their views, that must be done at the polls. My opinion is that you cannot always convince people who don't think like you to see your point of view. You are better off finding like-minded people who are already conditioned to see your point of view. I respect the challenges to the status quo, but I am not convinced that the status quo will be changed without a paradigm shift. That shift comes at the polls. I am convinced that the voting process provides us the mode for change.

Can you imagine the impact if we never missed an election? Voting matters and it is the process by which we get the change that we desire. If we are to convince our nation that black lives matter, it will be done by electing like-minded people. It's when we elect people who believe that black lives matter that we will see people acting as if black lives matter. But, as long as we continue to stay out of the process, we get similar results. People who are elected who do not believe that black lives matter reflect that in their policies and procedures. Voting is a voice that we have and we must use it—and use it regularly. It is far more important to vote in our local elections than our national elections. In fact, national midterm elections tend to have a greater impact on local politics than the presidential election. Yet, all voting cycles are important. Voting is a major responsibility because it is the way we exercise our voice. Ask yourself, how many men and women died for my right to vote? The fight was for the right *to* vote. It is important to understand the power and voice that we give up when we do not vote. Every election should be an opportunity to vote to protect black lives.

During my tenure in New York City, I was invited to breakfast with then-mayor Michael Bloomberg and his team to discuss police practices in the City of New York. The meeting with about ten community leaders and members of the mayor's staff was held at Gracie Mansion. As the only representative from Queens, I felt compelled to represent the voices of the many youth and adults of the borough. My statement to the mayor at that meeting was that policing in New York City for people of color felt more like something that was done to them and not for them. To say that the mayor was not pleased would be a significant understatement. The fact was that the mayor was trying to promote the positive benefits of the "stop and frisk" policy and my comments simply destabilized that notion. It was clear that he and I had a very different view of impact of "stop and frisk" as a policy of policing. While he clearly saw its merits he was totally unable to understand the negative impact of the policy on people of color.

At another gathering of ministers in Queens the mayor stated that "it's clear that you're more likely to get stopped in the city than I am; that's just how it is." The fact that he could "simply" pronounce the issue as a "matter of fact" was eye-opening to me. At that moment, it became abundantly clear that trying to get him to see life from the perspective of color was not going to happen.

The deep divide between perspectives in our society makes it very difficult to find common ground. Despite our differences, what unites us as Americans is our desire for freedom and equality. Even as we desire the same principles, our perspectives and positions force us to different conceptions. To this end, we become parochial in our view of life and its valuation. Our issue of valuation is as much about economics as it is about race. It is as much about history and heritage as ethnicity. It is as much about gender as it is about identity. We are too often willing to sort ourselves into categories, groups and communities to enhance our standing at the expense of the genuine desire for freedom and equality that we all seek. The result is that we become reactionary and unjust in our responses to the value of life.

If we are to convince black children and the broader society that black lives matter, we must be far more involved in the political process. Determining the leadership that will marshal us into a period of deepened valuation of life in America is essential. Voting in every election, participating in the community conversations and impacting not only the selection, but those who will enter consideration for selection will change the direction. Participating in the political process allows our voices to be heard and harnesses our ability to support like-minded candidates.

When we identify those like-minded voices we should support them in their work. Electing like-minded leaders and walking away from the process provides a void that is apt to be filled by anyone. Support like-minded leaders in their campaigns when possible, but more importantly once they take the mantel of leadership. Get involved in the process by getting to know your leadership, their views and policies. At the same time, confidently and boldly express your views and expectations as well.

To be clear, our participation should be in voting, involvement and engagement. We can all support the positive steps students make in their development. If you have children, go to as many games, programs, banquets, meets, or activities as you can. If you do not have children, develop a relationship with your local school, recreation center or church. Attend events as a spectator to encourage someone who has no one there. You can volunteer to work the time clock, read a book, sell snacks, or provide many other supportive functions that will help young people to begin to see and believe that their lives matter.

Protect Black Lives

Judgment Day

Chapter Eight

One of the basic tenants of our legal system is the importance of a juror of peers. The ability to get a fair trial is largely based on the make-up of the jury. Many attorneys spend hours selecting the "right" jury for trials in American courts. The jury is one of the most important aspects of the criminal justice system. Our system requires "peers" to consider the facts in legal cases and to determine the normal course of human engagement and interaction in our society.

Our peers are our neighbors and perhaps our friends; those who share the common experience of community in a common space. The expectation is not that we all see things the same, but perhaps we have a similar appreciation of some neighboring concepts and customs. Yet, as global as our society has become, there are still within our smaller communities cultural and societal norms that make up that community. The norm in Chicago can be dramatically different from Oak Park,

Illinois though they are but miles apart. The principle is that we get some common or communal understanding of the norm and what one normally could expect from the other. In our communities where diversity is great, the understanding of "the norm" is not as easy to ascertain. That is why the larger the pool, generally, the broader the community is represented. In other words, we all must do our part to inform the justice process by fully participating in it.

How many times do we avoid jury duty? To do so is to ignore the fact that the peer pool is changed every time we pass up a chance to sit in on a jury. It amazes me when grand jury after grand jury sends messages that are inconceivable and we are surprised and perhaps outraged. I suggest that we take a moment to consider the make-up of the jurors on the jury when we forgo our responsibility to participate in jury duty. I wonder how many of the outraged protesters in the city streets have given up the chance to perform this valuable service. As previously stated, it is very hard to get someone other than you to see you as you see yourself. It is even more challenging to convince your neighbor to think like you think and to act in your best interest.

Failure to participate in jury duty opens your seat up to someone with less to do with their time and perhaps a very different view or perspective about the things you think are important. When given a chance to serve on a jury take a moment to consider who will replace you and how will they view the facts of the case in your absence. I have never understood how a jury watching the Rodney King video decades ago could acquit that group of officers. One may have the same view of the Eric Garner video in New York or perhaps you can explain the two-second assessment in a recreation center park in Cleveland.

Jury duty plays an essential role in ensuring that black lives matter. Perspective is a huge scope from which we view everything in life and perhaps it gives clarity to the importance of life. We can continue to be surprised at the outcome of grand jury events or we can participate in the process of protecting life. It's not that we will pass judgment any differently, but at least you will know why the decision was deemed plausible. Like-minded persons cannot spend time outside of the process constantly wondering why the decisions constantly fail to reflect their views, opinions and perspectives. Perhaps the next time a jury duty form comes to your mailbox you will gladly, proudly and eagerly respond to the call and challenge. This will ensure that you bring your perspective to the process. You may even be surprised at what you learn and how you respond. But, be proactive and participate.

To ensure that black lives matter, we must take them seriously enough not to place judgment in the hands of someone else. There is a perspective and role that is unique to all of us and our participation raises the quality and standard of our system. In what many consider to be the greatest system of justice in the world, black lives fall on the dagger of malevolent justice. Our system is foundationally celebrated because it assumes that all lives are equally important and should be treated with blind application of justice. The participation in jury duty, testifying, and engaging improves our system as it rightly decrees that all lives matter.

*Lives Matter!*

*Chapter Nine*

I studied world religions while at Harvard and can attest that all of the major world religions value life. Life matters in Buddhism, Christianity, Hinduism, Islam and Judaism. The reality is that our faith doesn't divide us. Our humanity doesn't divide us. It is our perspective, ignorance and bigotry that divide us and devalue lives based on groups and complexion. Our collective goal should be to make it abundantly clear that all life matters. Black lives matter. Brown lives matter. White lives matter. All lives matter to God and should definitely matter to us. I am convinced that this is an ongoing task of ours and not one that will simply be conveyed in reaction to one event or another. Our collective responsibility is to ensure that our children understand that their lives matter and that all manner of life is valuable and must be preserved. This is our creed that we hold to be true and self-evident.

In the final analysis, my major and primary objective in this book is to emphatically make the point that our emergency response to crisis should be to remain proactive in developing our young people and inflating their personal valuation. We can make a difference by being involved all the time in some form or another and not just when "the crisis" occurs. There is an ongoing crisis that is occurring in our society and we need an ongoing response. It must be constant, cohesive and coordinated. I will work with whomever, wherever and whenever to ensure that our children are given a chance to succeed. It is clear to me that ALL LIVES MATTER; however, some do not appear to understand that black lives DO matter. I hope that you will be proactive in your home, church, community, and state to ensure that we build the personal valuation of black and brown students and to join with all like-minded people who truly believe that black lives matter and ultimately ALL LIVES MATTER!

# Black Men Respond:

## When did you realize your life mattered?

### Chapter Ten

As I completed this project I asked a few of my former students to answer the question—when did you realize your life mattered? The eleven stories that follow are their brief responses to the question. The responses range from personal to interpersonal. Some of the responses are very brief and some are not so brief. The young men represent a sample of the many young men that I have worked with over years and have achieved various levels of success in their lives. Some are married with children and others are still single. Some of the men in these stories are gainfully employed and building careers while others are still working to find their way in life. I hope that their stories will provide an impact and understanding of the complex issues relative to life as a young black man in America. Their stories are intended to make clear that men come to an understanding and realization that their lives have meaning at very different points.

I hope that you gain understanding from reading their responses. The work that we do with young men every day will impact the men they become. It is clear to me that we come to an understanding of our importance in life on very different terms. If we are to make the point that black lives matter, it is of great importance that we start that teaching with the very beings that will most benefit if we do and experience the greatest loss if we don't. Black lives, brown lives, white lives, and ultimately ALL LIVES MATTER and are worth saving and sustaining.

*I believe I always had a sense that my life mattered. When I was a child I wanted to become a pediatrician when I got older because I saw the importance of children for the future. Growing up experiencing life, I always analyzed how people moved, why people do the things they do whether they are bad or good. This analysis led me to always direct myself in a way that would be helpful to all of those around me who didn't understand what I saw. As the years passed my passion to be a help to others grew stronger. It led me to always try to do good by others because I understood that the world could be too cold at times. But I also saw how big of an affect simply smiling at someone and saying hello can have. Honestly, I always wondered how people could see the look of pain and distress in the faces of others and not try to do anything to help. This has led me to where I am today, steadily pressing on to my goal of reaching people in the most positive way. My greatest hope is to inspire others to do the same in their own way.*

JERMAINE, 26, Lead Multimedia Producer, NYC

*One of the greatest lessons I learned from Rev Quincy was that worship is a lifestyle. He taught that the Holy Spirit should so infect our lives that every part of our lives should be affected by Him. Through practical teaching, I learned how to live every day to the glory of God and this has transformed my life. This foundation is especially important for where I am in my current adventures in college. During these years God is bringing to light new gifts and giving me favor and mission in new regions of ministry such as fashion, photography, and film.*

TYRONE, 23, Student, Nyack, NY

*Life finally mattered when full awareness of the hidden mystery of the word of God took place within me (Ephesians 3:9, 1 Corinthians 4:1).*

*The consequences of a life devoid of pleasing God became immediately significant. Therefore, I began to care if I pleased God above pleasing others and most significantly above pleasing myself. My motivation for living changed. No longer was I caught up in what sustains us temporarily, but to grasping hold of what can sustain us eternally.*

*Many relate to the significance of life when their first-born child enters the world. Many anticipate and regard life when their marriage is fully consummated. Some even recognize life when their own depression is overcome as thoughts of suicide expire, giving rise to a newly developed self. Although I have personally endured all three scenarios and experienced much joy and satisfaction, none could compare to the solidification of knowing the mystery behind what no one but God can reveal. I could not call upon any reserves inside of me to gain this understanding because they simply were not there. I tried and I failed only to realize life only matters when it is of God.*

ORLANDO, 37, Sr. Software Engineer, Richmond, VA

*There have been two points in my life that the question of my life and what it means have arisen. The first occurred late one evening in summer of 2002; I sat in a dark room with no electricity, no food, no money, and no people to turn to for help. The enemy whispered in my ear that it was better to take my own life to escape. I was a victim of my own sin and the enemy was trying to complete his task. At that moment, God spoke to me very clearly and said that I have more for you and that I should return home. At that moment I chose life because God told me that death was not the path He laid out for me.*

*The second reinforcement upon the fact that my life mattered was in 2008 when my first son was born. I loved him. Becoming a father made me appreciate the love that God had for His Son and the sacrifice He made. It reminded me that my life was important because I was here to pour into him, to build him and to guide him. This is a reflection I have made each time my wife and I have been blessed with another child.*

RASHAD, 33, Lead Program Analyst, US Dept. of Homeland Security, TSA, Threat Assessment Division, Washington, DC

*I realized my life mattered when I began to put the lives of others before my own--mainly children. A child has a way of making you feel smarter, stronger, and braver than you are. I am all of those things to the children because God's light shines through me and reflects on them. My life matters because God makes it matter. My purpose is defined by the lives that I touch each day, and I realize that in every breath I take.*

AUBREY, 31, Children's Leader, NYC

*I realized my life mattered at the age of 12. I used to get in trouble a lot. My mother was tired of it. She would constantly discipline me and even pray about it. One Sunday night at The Assembly Church of God there was a baptism going on. As I sat there and watched my friend Nigel get baptized, I got a feeling within to get baptized too. While in the water Pastor Yateman asked me if I had anything to say before I was baptized. I said, I will try really hard to change my life. Right after I came up from the water I realized two things. The first was that I being baptized was one of the happiest moments in my mother's life (as she shed tears). Second, was that God has a purpose for me and my life really mattered.*

JOE, 36, Construction Representative, NYC


*I realized that my life mattered when I went to homecoming two years after graduating from college. While catching up with some friends they told me how grateful they were to have me as friend. At the time they didn't think much about it but now they appreciated the advice I gave during hard times, the constant encouragement and for praying with them when they needed someone to pray with. It was during those moments at homecoming that I realized I mattered because just being myself affected my friends in a positive way.*

CAMERON, 24, School Psychologist, Long Island, NY

*I realized life mattered when I went to college in the Midwest and I was the only black drummer in all my music classes, before I left to do a semester at University of Wisconsin, Stevens Point. Rev. was called to spread the word of God to youth who needed Christ in another city. When he left New York I thought more about the fact he wasn't here, not remembering his explanation on the understanding of his sermons living in Christ eyes. I realized when those who speak about the love of God and speak about what He has done for them share—you must listen.*

*"Fear loves the weak." I realize when people motivate you do great, listen. God is love and with all the hate in the world you can't be afraid. I was blessed to have learned wisdom from Rev Quincy. It's better to give than to receive; love is the key; you can't always take the easy way out when things get hard; you must fight through and pray; prayer is the key to survival on earth until the Lord makes you an angel in heaven; and the music you listen to determines your growth in Christ. As a musician, I've learned that negativity in lyrics takes you away from your relationship with Christ. Yet, when you listen to music and His word, life is good. You have the courage to grow when you listen to the Lord's music.*

BERNARD, 22, Student, NYC

*The day I knew my life mattered was on a hot summer day in 1999. I was 19-years-old and just started going to church. I had one foot in the Word and the other still firmly planted in the world. One day, while on the corner of Murdock Ave and 199th Street, I was about to get into a world of trouble when a black Saturn made an illegal U-turn and pulled up to the curbside. Of course, my first inquiry was "when did cops start driving Saturns?" However, it wasn't the cops at all; it was Rev. Quincy, who abruptly told me to get into the car. From that point, we drove around all day helping others—visiting the sick, moving furniture in an elderly assistance home, and just doing good things for complete strangers. This, of course, was the exact opposite of what I was doing before I got in his car. Rev saw an opportunity to take me with him to do things I may have never done without his example being set for me to follow. It was then that I realized that my life really doesn't matter unless I help others realize the value of their own lives. Currently, I do this through service, which has proven to be the greatest and most effective form of ministry with young people. Helping people is ingrained in me and I attribute that all to the relationship I built with Rev. Quincy.*

CHARLES, 34, Team Lead, Henrico, VA

*It was April 30, 2012, a bright sunny Monday morning better than most Mondays. Unlike every other 17 year old, I wasn't in class. I was on my way to my aunt's to join her on her drive to pick up my cousin, who had completed the year at Howard University. I had been out of school for nearly a month due to my mischief at school. When I arrived at my aunt's house she and my little cousin were taking everything out of the car so that we would have room for the luggage. As we departed my aunt asked me to make sure my little cousin's seat belt was on. Our next stop was a quick stop to purchase a navigation device for the trip. That is what I remember prior to the most devastating moment of my life. I had fallen asleep and woke up to my aunt's haunting screams. As I braced for the impact of the SUV as it flipped from the right lane to the middle divider on the New Jersey Turnpike, I prepared for the end. My aunt and I survived but, my eight year old cousin was ejected and airlifted to a local hospital. After her passing, I realized that my life mattered and my childish behavior as a teen was reflected in the loss of her innocent life. This was my wake-up call and the moment I realized that my life mattered and I had a second chance to take life seriously.*

MAURICE, 20, Security Officer, NYC

*Why do I exist? Why did God choose me? How did I get here? For what purpose, was I created? We periodically ask ourselves these questions, determined to find the answers on a day by day basis as we witness the events that may either directly or indirectly impact our lives. It is evident, that our society faces challenges, obstacles and occurrences that capture our attention every day. Therefore, as we bear witness to these events that unfold around us, it becomes clear that it's not a question of "if", but rather "when", the aforementioned questions are asked. At times it may be a child that has been abducted, a teen that has been misguided or an adult whose life has been destroyed through some tragic act. Events that have left us baffled and distraught. But then there are those positive and extraordinary occurrences that take place like a medical marvel or an inventive discovery or a technological upgrade or even a historical feat that may pose a second series of questions, including the ever important, "How too, can I make a difference?" And of course, the more intimate and personal challenges we face, cannot be omitted. Often we wake up, meticulously plan our day, play out our plans and return to our safe haven, not even recognizing the "bullets" of life's "loaded gun" that have missed us….until it happens. Unfortunately it is only then that most of us really realize that our lives matter.*

*It was Friday, August 8, 2008, I was preparing for my attendance at a wedding. But first, errands had to be run. As the time for me to end my personal list of things to do drew closer, I found myself rushing and cutting corners in order to remain on schedule. At approximately 4pm, I was involved in a motorcycle accident that should've been fatal…I walked away. Bruised and lacerated, but ALIVE. The first respondent on the scene, an off duty police officer, checked me out and reassured me that I will be okay. Ironically, I learned months later that this same officer would succumb to his injuries in a motorcycle accident and tragically die. Although I was saddened, I immediately recognized that the Lord granted mercy on my life once again. It was then that I recognized the expectations that have been placed on my life from HIM. It was then that I realized my life really mattered. The lives that our Creator created matters... Jesus' life mattered...sisters and brothers, YOUR LIFE MATTERS!*

ANDREW, 33, Youth Leader, NYC

# Epilogue

Mere days before the first printing of this book another three young black men were gunned down in a barber shop just blocks away from our church in Cleveland. One was a husband and father of two. The random act of violence was not perpetrated by law enforcement, but another act of "black on black" crime. The senseless act devastated six families directly and several communities indirectly. The impact of these violent acts on the families and communities involved leave deep emotional and psychological wounds that are very difficult to repair. That is not to mention the financial impact to the wife of the slain owner and his children. Whatever the make-up of the situation, it deeply impacts lives that matter.

Imagine the impact on the children who watch the news or perhaps frequent that shop or the many shops attached. They are bound to be left with questions and fears that haunt them. One bystander questioned "where are the marches for these young men?" I was reminded of the purpose of this book. One hundred or one thousand marchers, protesters or mourners standing outside that shop could not bring back to these families any of the lives lost. Yet, our individual and collective efforts daily to increase the personal and collective valuation of black lives go a long way to saving lives that which would have otherwise been lost.

What if someone would have convinced the shooter that black lives mattered and had value? What if we could convince a generation of young black men that their lives matter and in fact so do the lives of their classmates and neighbors? This must start in our personal circles of influence today. We cannot wait for another program to launch. We cannot wait for additional legislation to be enacted. We cannot wait for the right man or woman to be elected. We must within our own circles of influence build a movement that states unequivocally that black lives matter—in fact ALL LIVES MATTER!